RE-
THINK

ReThink your life's strange events.

Michael J. O. Michael

Edition v.1.1

CONTENTS

INTRODUCTION

When I became aware of the similarity between my life's events and those reported by UFO contactees and abduction reports, I decided to probe deeper into possible correlations.

My subsequent studies revealed that some UFO investigators withhold publishing selected information specifically to help validate future reports from the field. The rationale being that field investigations will sometimes include details that are known only to investigators. And those details sometimes occur across multiple reported events, and when it does, it helps validate those events as genuine because those details have never been publicly available.

In more than one instance, my life experiences paralleled those not usually published in print, according to some UFO investigators and authors.

One such example was brought to my attention when an author revealed that some people suspected of encounters with UFOs had mentioned reading languages that they had never learned. Sometimes their reading took the form of a massive and rapid influx of information, placed directly into their mind; causing a sort of super-reading to occur. Researchers have described it as "downloading." (I will detail my related experience a little later.)

In another example of similarity between my life's events and those reported by UFO contactees, I was shocked to read that some people filing abduction reports also reported unexplained flesh wounds on the feet. I too had such an injury that I'd never been able to explain. (I also detail my related experience a little later.)

When I read those kinds of things in several UFO related books, it became clear that my experiences were not unique. I also realized many people who have had similar experiences, that they could not adequately explain, might benefit as I have, from knowing about the information in UFO and related studies. I connected many events in my life with the experiences of others in ways I never would have considered if not for my exposure to new information.

So, I decided to write about my life's events and to share how they paralleled many reported incidents in the literature of the UFO community, and to the scientific research related to quantum physics.

By writing about my "weird" experiences, I can

share them with others and hopefully encourage others to gain insight into the true nature of events in their life, and perhaps bring closure to some of those experiences. Of course, doing so may simultaneously bring many more questions. But even so, the isolation that previously existed may be reduced by knowing others share some of these life-events.

The goal of my writing this little book is deliberate and straightforward. It is to help others reconsider their experiences in a new light of modern thinking. Specifically, by "modern thinking," I am referring to the new scientific information, and equally important, the new attitudes reflected in currently published materials dealing with a variety of topics. Those topics include quantum physics, UFOs (or UAPs as they are now being referred to), abductee experiences, consciousness studies, and related articles.

I hope to encourage you and others to "rethink" if perhaps you, too, have had events in your life, worthy of renewed consideration as something other than dreams or imaginings.

For many years, I have considered many of the events I write about in this book to be "...too real to be dreams, and too weird to be real..." However, research has convinced me that there may be much more to some of the events than I previously realized. And, this newfound information has given me a new viewpoint. I now know that I am not alone, and that many others have also had very similar life experiences.

If you have had experiences that have been tucked away as part of your life that you have not been able to fully dismiss as having not really happened, yet felt uneasy discussing because the events were just too weird to be real, then this little book might open a new world of possibilities for you.

If this work helps even one individual to find answers or possible explanations for the previously unexplainaible things they have expereinced, then I have succeeded.

I welcome hearing from you about your experiences. You are welcome to write to me through my website: **www.michaeljomichael.com**.

COWBOYS AND INDIANS

I was born in an era when not everyone even owned a television. TVs were only black and white, and ours sported a "huge" screen that was about 11 inches corner to corner. TV shows included many cowboys and Indian shows, which were very popular when I was a kid. So, clearly, I could have easily dreamed about cowboys and Indians. However, I don't remember ever dreaming about either.

What I do remember, however, was an experience that occurred when I was very young. I am guessing that I was three or four years old. I don't think I was yet in kindergarten, and if I were, I would have been about five years old.

One morning I awoke with a very vivid memory, not dissimilar to experiences I would have many times later in my early adulthood.

Upon awakening in the morning, I had a vivid and clear memory of waking earlier that morning in early pre-dawn dim light to see the walls of my house were semi-transparent, as was the floor and ceiling. They were there, but I could see through them, and they had a faded, grey, look.

As I looked through the transparent walls, there, walking toward me were three figures, a cowboy, an Indian, and a pilot (or some military person).

This event is unmistakable in my mind. There was an associated sense of presence and importance attached to this event that has lasted throughout my entire life. Another thing that I can remember is that these entities took me somewhere. I can't recall where. I remember them taking me out the backdoor of my house. Later I was returned to the sofa where I had been sleeping.

They were there to get me or talk with me, or something. In any case, those three were approaching because *I* was there. I was the focus of interest. That is all I remember about the experience. I am not sure why I had been sleeping on the sofa that night.

TIGHTLY TUCKED

Soon after that experience with the three visitors, my parents were planning for me to sleep on the sofa again. My dad decided to tuck my blanket around me and under the frontside and backside edges of the sofa's cushions. He tucked me in so tightly that I could barely work my arms out from underneath the blanket. After a while, I was able to get free and go to sleep. Nothing unusual occurred that night, unlike the previous time when I had the visitation.

The next day, my mother and father were discussing something or other, and the topic of me being tucked-in so tightly came up, perhaps because I was complaining about the blanket being "too tight". Dad responded by telling mom that he had tucked me in real snugly, so I wouldn't "get out and hide again."

Then he went on to explain that the previous night, (the night I had the visitation), that he'd gotten up in the middle of the night for some reason, and checked on me. But to his surprise, he said that, I wasn't on the sofa and that he couldn't find me! He'd searched the house for me out of concern, and never located me. I remember thinking that he seemed upset as he recanted the experience.

Perhaps he was even angry with me because he seemed to think I was hiding from him in the middle of the night. He implied I intentionally didn't respond when he called out for me. I also remember feeling very much like 'that's not true" even though I was rather young. That was the end of the matter, but it left me with a genuine feeling of having been falsely accused.

Why couldn't he find me!
Where was I?
Was I with the three visitors?
Why would he give-up looking for me?

None of those thoughts occurred as a child, but as an adult, those thoughts have occurred. These events have taken on new possible implications along with others described below.

Growing up, I mostly considered the three-visitors experience to be just a vivid dream, however, it was the first of many expereinces that seemed too real in many ways to be a dream, even a vivid one. And my dad's complaint about me 'hiding' was some-thing that, although weird, I never really thought about that much as a kid. That was until I read reports by other people about entities that can reportedly assume different appearances and shapes, at will. I'd probably blow the experience off as a dream, were it not for the fact that I've had many experiences with a similar level of "weirdness." For that reason, I've included it as my earliest memory of an event that seems, now over 50 years later, to have a weightiness and significance to it. One that far surpasses what "on the surface" makes up the content of the recollection itself.

STAR-BODIED NIGHTIME VISITORS

A few years later, I am guessing that I was probably about eight or nine years old when I had a very distinct event occur. This time I was old enough to realize that it was something extremely unusual.

I was lying in my bed, on a Sunday evening. The bedroom had two doorways. The first doorway, near the headboard of the bed, connected my bedroom to the living room. The second doorway connected my room to a large room in the back of the home.

As I lie in my bed, I had not yet fallen asleep. My mother and father were in the living room watching television, and I can recall that my mother was also talking on the telephone.

As I gazed towards the darkened second doorway towards the foot of the bed, I saw something quite startling.

In the doorway, which was wholly dark, it was as if there was a shadow in the darkness. It's a little bit difficult to describe, but there was what appeared to be mostly the outline of a human-like form, very tall, filling the entire doorway. There were no features in this humanlike-shaped "shadow." Oddly the space occupied by the shadow was filled with what looked to me to be tiny little starlike sparkles.

What I was observing was a doorway, completely dark, within which appeared an even more mysterious form in a human-like shape. It was tall filling the entire door-frame area, having no discernible features. And it seemed as if filled with tiny points of light much like small little stars in a moonless night's sky.

I saw this "entity" on several occasions as a part of several of these experiences. I cannot recall how many times, although it seems like at least three or four times, and I do not believe it was more than five or six. I think these occurred between the ages of eight or nine to about ten to twelve years of age.

At the time this was very, very puzzling to me. As an adult I find it interesting that I was never frightened by the experience as a child. I recall that I may have told a friend, but cannot remember whom. But I do recall pondering the experience at great length.

At the time, I named them the "star people." However, there was never anything to the experience beyond the shape and the 'stars' filling it. There was never movement or any other attributes or inter-action associated with the shape. The expereince was not unlike the feeling one has when, as a child, an authority figure, like a teachcr, is present with you, but not interactive beyond monitoring you, and (so it seemed) providing some level of protec-tion.

I could not have known the long history of similar experiences, especially among prehistoric peoples, that they have recorded, often as petroglyphs.

CYLINDER-SHAPED OBJECT

My community elementary school consisted of grades kindergarten through fifth grade. During this time, in what I guess was the second through the 4th-grade timeframe, I saw a UFO.

It was a clear day on the playground. I was at recess, and I think it was later in the school year, or early in the school year, in Michigan, because the weather was reasonably mild but fresh, similar to either a spring or autumn day's weather. I was standing facing south, and gazing up into the sky. As I recall, I was standing by myself, holding onto the chain-link fence looking skyward. There were many school-mates around me, but none were looking at what I was.

Above me, almost directly overhead, I distinctly remember watching a cylinder-shaped object sitting motionless in the sky. I knew it was not a blimp, nor a balloon. It was metallic-looking. Even at that age, I had an excellent aircraft awareness, and this was no airplane.

I do not remember any strong reaction other than gazing up and wondering what it might have been. I did not think of it as a UFO, because at that age, I had no UFO vocabulary. I was well aware of airplanes, and maybe of rockets, but that was about it for airborne machines. I knew it was neither of those, so I remember just watching it sitting up there in the sky, silent and motionless.

I seem to recall that I pointed it out to a fellow student who gave it little notice. What does linger in my memory very strongly is a sense of bewilderment that I did not know what the object or craft was.

I may have heard the term "flying saucer," but the memory of the event does not include thinking in those terms at all. All I remember is what it looked like, the fact that it was very high and motionless, and knowing that it was unnatural and non-ordinary.

Eventually, the recess ended, and I headed back into the school. I wondered if I should tell my teacher about the craft I had observed. I did not.

I had no idea about UFOs or anything of the kind, but the experience is as vivid today as it was over 50 years ago. When I became an adult and saw my first cylinder-shaped UFO image, my memory darted back to the day I saw one of them as a kid.

UFO abductees and other encounters often occur

over many years, and it is not unusual for encounters to begin at a very young age. The three-visitors experience in the previous chapter and this experience are noteworthy because they were the first experiences of many, and they ocurred when I was rather young, as is the case of with many experiencers.

FEARFUL WALK

This event, too, may not have been particularly noteworthy on its own as an isolated event, were it the only one of its kind, but it was not. It is included here because of the powerful sense of a "presence" that accompanied it. And not just because of that alone, but because of how similar that presence was, to other similar "presence-sense" experiences that would occur later in my life.

I think I was between 11 and 13 years of age when this event occurred. Walking home from my buddy's house one starry late summer or early fall evening, I had an intense sense of being followed. The feeling included a sense of being observed in a very tangible way. I did not feel that it was from behind me. What made the experience weird and scary was that the threat seemed to be coming from *above* me. I recall that I looked up, above me, not glancing about me or behind me because there was a powerful sense that the danger was "up there," not at ground level.

I distinctly remember being thoroughly upset by that aspect of being scared from above, that is, the sensation of looking up, not around, for the menace.

I increased my pace, and broke into a run, nearly panicked. I avoided looking up again and ran home as fast as I could. The safety of my house wrapped around me as I entered. There was a very real sense that being inside somehow blocked the feeling of being observed.

I wondered why I was unable to see anything above me except the night sky, especially with such a strong sense of something "up there" interested in me.

But all I could see was an incredibly clear moonless starry Michigan night's sky.

INTERLUDE

The preceding paragraphs are my recollections of early childhood events. At the time, they were just events. Odd, but mixed-in the other activities of youth, seldom thought about, but never totally forgotten. It would be decades before they would resurface with possible explanations that were impossible to imagine at the times they happened.

In the paragraphs that follow, I describe non-determinant but notable events that occurred in my early adult life, across a few years with little to no other significant events. I refer to this period as *the interlude period.*

During the interlude period, I would be unaware that at least one of the experiences during that time would eventually surface later as a pivotal experience.

After this "interlude" period, a plethora of experiences would unfold during an intense period spanning several years.

OLD HOUSE CONVERSATION

I had moved into an old house under some odd circumstances. Upon inquiring about a rental house, the rental agent informed me that the home was involved in a legal battle between its owner and the city. The water supply had been interrupted, and the city wanted to declare the property condemned. The city was trying to say the property was condemned but couldn't do so if a tenant was resident there. The matter was in court proceedings. The agent offered me a deal. I could live in the home free of charge until the legal case resolved. My residency would stay the condemnation ruling, and, allow time for the water issues to resolve, thus beating the condemnation ruling.

The bathroom, consisting of a sink and toilet, did have running water. The water for the toilet and drain still functioned, although the water seemed to always be at natural temperature, and not heated in any way, consequently, it would freeze during winter.

I agreed to the deal because I was not making a lot of money in those days. Having me as an occupant did delay the house condemnation because the city's laws prevented a house being designated as condemned if it had an occupant.

One afternoon, late, maybe 4 or 5 PM, I had an immense feeling that something or someone was observing me from above the house. The atmosphere became filled with tremendous anxiety over the next hour or so. And then, to my amazement, sounds from the roof began occurring. It sounded as if someone or something was moving around on the rooftop. Whatever was making the noises were, or seemed to be rather large. My intuition suggested a significant-sized person or one or more animals.

By this time it was dark, very dark.

Over the next hour or two, the sound continued. There was also a powerful sense of being watched or observed, by something that was "up there."

At first I listened, then eventually, I spoke loudly upward and began to yell toward the ceiling and roof to scare off whatever was moving around up there. After no change, I threatened shooting through the roof. Still no change.

I became so concerned for my safety, that eventually I grabbed my .22 caliber rifle and fired a few rounds straight through the ceiling, in several places. After that, the sounds of movement above me ceased.

The intense sensation of being observed did not cease, however. It became even more intense.

Then to my amazement, I had the clear and distinct sensation that I could have communication with that something or someone responsible for all the commotion! There weren't any audible sounds or anything tangible. But apparent specific thoughts were occurring as if spoken by whoever, or whatever was "up there."

Telepathy? Perhaps. I have no idea, but I can affirm that for the next hour or so, I was having a two-way conversation. I would speak aloud, and the other side of the exchange would reply, directly into some part of my mind that understood the reply.

Weird? Yes. Very. I know that now, and I fully understood that then. But strange as it was, it was happening, nonetheless.

Eventually, the message was clear. It was "...don't be afraid... nothing is going to harm you," I replied aloud, "What do you want, what are you?"

The "dialog" from that point went on for the better part of an hour. I don't remember much about the detail of the conversation. What I do recall is me asking "it" to leave, and leave me alone.

Eventually, I had an unambiguous sense of "... no intention to alarm you, no harm intended." And just as abruptly as it had started, the "conversation" was over, and I had the very assured sense of once again being alone.

This expereince took place while I was wide-awake in the late afternoon or early evening, and lasted quite a while.

Contact? Maybe. Contact with what or whom? I have no idea.

That kind of event only occurred once and has never reoccurred since.

STICKY CLOCK

While still living in that rent-free and water-free home, one more weird event would occur before I moved out. And unlike the conversation event which had no further impact on my future life, this next event would be instrumental as a pivot point in my life several years later.

I was working a split shift, starting at 8 PM and ending around 4 AM. I was a computer operator at a major banking and defense data-center. I liked working the split shift. I enjoyed the quiet time after my shift ended and the early hours of the next day when I could conduct any business or other activities. I would go to sleep around 10 AM to noon to prepare for my next shift. I usually set the alarm on my alarm clock radio to wake me up around 5 or 6 pm.

On two or three occasions, I had the most remarkable and unexplainable experience.

On those occassions, when the alarm sounded, I would awaken, or so it seemed, and look at the time on the clock. And reaching over to press down on the snooze button, my hand seemed to go right through the clock! This experience shocked and startled me. The first time this had happened, I quickly withdrew my hand from the clock that it seemed to be "inside."

That is, I tried to withdraw my hand. But I could not!

My hand was somehow enmeshed or entangled with the radio alarm clock itself. The sensation was like trying to pull my hand out of a strong magnetic force holding it in place. Eventually, I was able to free it, and it was quickly released.

Immediately I was fully awake.

I wondered what had just happened and if the experience was just a very intense dream, although I seemed to be completely awake. Or was I in an altered not-awake and not-asleep state-of-consciousness, just before emerging into my normal awake state?

I mused over this experience several times as it was very, very odd and captured my interest.

This "sticky clock" experience occurred a couple more times, maybe two or three. On one of those occasions as I attempted to pull my hand back, I was able to pull back from the clock, but my hand stayed entangled with it. Consequently, my arm seemed to "stretch" to the length necessary as I moved away from the alarm clock.

Weird? Yes, very weird.

It took a lot of effort to "pull away" from the clock, and when I did get free, my elongated arm seemed to "snap" back to my body with a jolt and a "clicking sound."

These were bizarre, authentic, non-dream state experiences. They seemed to be happening in a fully alert, fully conscious state of mind, albeit an altered state of consciousness of some kind.

Throughout this period, I was maintaining a full-time job. And at times attending college part-time, was in good health both physically and mentally as well as emotionally.

It would be a few years before I found out that the sticky clock sort of experience was not limited to me. And that the state of consciousness I had experienced during them was known to exist in at least two other documented events.

Eventually, I discovered my experiences described as part of out-of-body experiences or an OOBE. But at the time these things were occurring, I had never heard the term OOBE, and had no awareness of anything of the sort.

Eventually, the legal battle over the little house resolved. The owner restored water and told me rent payments were required. I moved out. After leaving the condemned house, there was a period of a few years, where little out of the ordinary happened.

But the quiet time would end abruptly during a bicycle trip to a campground in middle Michigan.

BAY CITY

Growing up, my roommate and I both had lived on the same street, a couple of blocks from one another, and grew up in the same neighborhood, and attended the same high school. We were a couple of hard-working young men. And we were hippies. In those days you could be both, a hippie, and a professional worker, a blue-collar worker, a student or a professor, even a doctor.

It was 1974, and I held a full-time job and worked every day. I attribute my focus on working and providing for myself financially, as part of my blue-collar upbringing. I was the hippie and computer operator in a sizeable commercial computer center. At that time, that facility was called a "data center." My data center was a medium-sized banking and defense-industry computer center.

I held top-secret security clearance. Many times I ran the computer results analysis programs on data gathered from White Sands missile base and testing facility. The nation's first computer-ballot election results were trusted to me for operations with a full cadre of TV reporters on hand.

And although I didn't know it at the time, in a few short years, I would appear on the cover of _Computer World_ magazine. A featured article on cascaded networked terminals for a large travel company, a first in its day, included me as a featured subject.

While the "hippie" part of my lifestyle said one thing, at 24 years old, my career was already exciting and something I took rather seriously. And I was doing very well on the job. I was in excellent physical condition due in part to extensive cycling activity, and mentally on-my-game, with no emotional challenges other than those appearing in any healthy heterosexual single male of the time.

In all ways, I was physically and mentally a fine specimen of a healthy, hard-working, smart fellow. So was my roommate. If ever we had to provide testimony to a court, we'd be believable and credible witnesses.

In 1973 my roommate and I, were avid cyclists. Many days we would ride to work, and we both rode nearly every day and night. We rode bicycles just for sheer enjoyment. I can remember what it felt like flying along on two wheels. Now that I am well into my senior years, I appreciate the great health I had in those days. I was so physically fit that the physical challenges of hard-riding were virtually non-consequential, and riding was a lot like flying. It was effortless.

Eventually, my roommate and I decided to take a bi-cycle road-trip, and our training for the trip started in the spring. By the mid-summer, we were strapping 5 or 6 finishing bricks to our bikes, along with a six-pack of beer, and would take off to find the most challenging inclines and routes possible.

We both had rock-like physiques by the time the fall season came around. Our road trip from just north of Detroit, Michigan, to the Bay City State Park, was approaching quickly.

We had about 110 miles ahead of us, and as it turned out, we spent two days to get there.

We were there together for a few days; then my roommate continued on his bike for another few hundred miles north. I stayed at the camp in Bay City till the end of the week and planned to cycle southward back home at the end of the week.

I could not have known then that the next day or two would be life-affecting. I didn't fully understand it until over forty years later.

By the time my buddy left the campsite, It was very late in the camping season at the state park. There were several areas in the park available to campers. The camping area closest to the park office was the one where we had camped. A road of several hundred feet ran from the park office, through a set of campsites to where we pitched our tents. After several days our camping together was finished and my roommate headed north to continue his longer bicycle trek, leaving me behind alone.

The park's campground we were in had emptied of all campers except me. I was the only camper in that camping area.

Regardless of my tip-top physical condition, by my last night in Bay City, I was already starting to dread the ride home alone. I remember the emptiness around me because I was the only camper left in my camp area. It was me, and a couple of hundred empty campsites surrounding me.

The road ran about a quarter-mile from my campsite to the park office. From the campsite, the road made a 90-degree turn to the right, and after another quarter mile, intersected the main road. Past the main road was the beach that ran around the bay on all sides except the northern portion where the bay opens up into one of Michigan's great lakes.

I remember trying to get warm my last night at the campsite, as fall was enveloping me in my tiny pup-tent. Closing my eyes, I was thinking about how I dreaded the ride back to my home in Ferndale, although I was glad I was going home.

I realized I hadn't walked over to the beach, and I think I walked over to check out the bay before turning in for the night. I say "I think" I walked to the beach, because I am not really sure about that, as will be explained a little bit later.

34

Regardless of a beach-walk, or not, eventually I closed my eyes and drifted into a deep sleep.

HARD AWAKENING

I awoke the next morning as if resurrected from the dead. I felt drugged. Heavy. Murky, even sedated. For someone in as great physical shape as I was, this feeling of utter incapacitation was most troubling.

Never had I felt like I felt that morning. Up till then, I had never experienced anesthesia. I would later in my life liken how I felt that morning to waking from an anesthesiologist's deep-sleep cocktail.

Helping my body back to feeling normal took a long time that morning. I couldn't remember the preceding evening with clarity, and I felt so lousy that the lack of clear memory didn't occur to me as something to be questioned.

The empty campground I went to sleep in, also had changed during the night. Upon awakening, I realized that a single camper in a small pickup truck had parked directly across from my campsite sometime in the night after I had fallen asleep. He was already awake, too, and waved from his site to me.

I waved back but was thinking that I felt so bad I hoped he left me alone.

The sedated numbness that had permeated my mind was only half of the morning's challenge.

Immediately upon waking up, I had a profound memory about part of my night. It was just a fragment of a memory during a short time in the middle of the night. It was troubling me because I couldn't remember anything before, or after, this section of the night that I could remember, and that ever so vividly.

The emotions around this middle-of-night memory was a mixture of exhilarated, awestruck, confused, and rethinking, for many years to come.

This memory of what seemed to be an authentic experience occurring during the night was extraordinarily vivid.

That memory was as follows; with no idea how I got there, there I was, standing in what looked like the bridge, or central control area, of someplace filled with very technical equipment. It was an area like the bridge of a ship, perhaps an aircraft carrier or nuclear sub, or the cockpit or an aircraft, or spacecraft. Somewhere important, to be sure.

The place was not very tall, and I remember having to hunch-down a little so as to clear the "ceiling".

And whatever the craft was, where it was, was unquestionable and soon to be apparent. It was hanging somewhere in the depths of space, outer space to be precise.

I was in a tight area, and after a brief moment, not unlike waking up suddenly, I became aware of standing "there", when someone or something "spoke" to me, seemingly telepathically, from behind me, from the darker areas around me. I never saw the speaker.

The "voice," seemingly male, said, "Go ahead and step forward a little."

The space in front of me was somewhat dark only extended about 1 or 2 feet in front of me. The ceiling and floor seemed to each taper down to meet and form the "wall" in front of me. I could sense it was the side of the craft, or minimally a wall of some kind.

Someone's foot or a piece of gear on the floor caused me to slightly stumble, as I started to step a little forward, as instructed by the "voice" from behind me. Just as I put up my hand to break my forward fall against the craft's wall, -it disappeared!

Specifically, at the point where the arcing floor and ceiling met in front of me, and proceeding backward toward me, both above my head and below my feet, -vanished, becoming completely transparent.

I reflexively jolted backward to avoid "falling out."

Then I realized I could still place my hand on the surfaces to support myself so I could lean forward and look *through* them, I could touch them, but I couldn't see them. They were clear as crystal.

Outside the craft and below at about a forty-degree angle, there was an incredible spiral-shaped spectacle taking place.

I didn't know what it was exactly, a spiral-galaxy, or something equally marvelous. It was gigantic. More beautiful than anything I'd ever seen. Unimaginable, indescribable. I also remember a strong feeling of surprise watching the spirals rotating from the center of the object outward, in the opposite direction that I expected them to, based on their appearance.

The persons or beings there with me seemed to be responsible for my being on-board, and also appeared to be the ones in control of the craft's operation, and the situation.

They seemed to be communicating to me; "We wanted you to see this, it is rare to be able to show this, to show it in the making." I did not then, and do not now know what precisely I was observing. But it was clear my hosts were referring to the spiral object below us in space; the one I was watching through invisible walls.

The observance was one of the most potent life events I have had.

Was I supposed to remember or forget that experience when I awoke? Or was I supposed to forget whatever had happened before and after this observance-event, but had been "awakened" so I would remember this, but, this only?

I may never know the answers to those questons, but I do know that the extraordinary and vivid memory seemed to conflict with the massive sense of being sedated when I woke up.

DRIVER FROM NOWHERE

The fantastic view of the stellar object and the whole experience of being there seemed to end in an instant, and the very next moment I was awake inside my tent. I was waking up, transitioning from the encounter to the normal waking state, or trying to. Several minutes later, as I was trying to clear my head, my new "neighbor" was walking over to introduce himself.

I don't remember what we said. It just wasn't remarkable. But what was unusual was that this guy was telling me that he was going to drive directly to my final destination. And he offered to drive me home!

I found that to be in the "a little weird" category and initially refused the favor.

There I was in an empty campground, and in a section closed for the season. Other parts of the camp were still open. This guy arrives during the night and parks directly across from me when the whole section is vacant and available. He has a pickup truck with an empty bed. He says he is going to the exact intersection I have as my final destination. He offers to drive me home. Yes, a little weird!

Even though I was dreading the return trip alone, I said: "no, thanks." Maybe I overvalued my independence and was also a bit untrusting.

Between the two of us, we had enough beer to down a few. So we did. We got to know each other while drinking beer for breakfast. Later that afternoon, we threw my camping gear and bike into the back of the pickup, and a few hours later, I was dropped off at home. The unnamed driver from nowhere returned to nowhere, and just as abruptly as he'd appeared in my world, he left.

Was he placed there to ensure my safe return home? If so, by whom or what? Was there something that had happened to me while on the craft that required I be kept safe and secure? Why had he picked that one campsite out of hundreds of empty sites that night? Was he going where I was precisely going that day?

I had many questions about my providentially provided ride; however, they eventually faded, but never totally disappeared, even to this day.

Never did I think of these events in terms of aliens, UFOs, or anything like that. For the most part, I thought of them as unusual, maybe extremely vivid dreams. But the events, especially being inside the craft, remained an order of "reality" more real than any dream I'd ever had, and just below the threshold of what seems like everyday reality.

At that time, the events seemed to be very real, but different from my everyday waking reality. After many years, they still seem to be a kind of our reality, unlike ordinary consciousness but very real just the same. Maybe there are many aspects to one's existence. Perhaps those experiences were not separate realities, but different views of one truth.

The bike trip had taken place in the fall. By the time spring started, some internal changes were emerging within me. These changes came "out of nowhere." Until that time, I had never thought in terms of the sort of lifestyle changes coming at me full-steam.

I had been a beer-drinking, cigarette, and pot-smoking hippy computer guy. Now, after the Bay City trip, things were changing. Changes that seemed like excellent ideas were accompanied by the necessary attitudes, energy, and commitment to succeed at making very significant lifestyle changes.

The idea of "going clean" to experience "me" at my absolute physical, mental, and even spiritual best seemed like something I must do. I didn't know why.

There was a strong sense emerging that I also

needed to clean up parts of my life that were not physical. They included my thought life, my moral outlook and actions, and so forth. Fundamentally, for reasons unknown, I was compelled to reinvent myself from the inside out.

In the post-craft-experiences of Bay City, it was as if I found myself touched by a powerful life-change agent of some kind. A necessary change was upon me. It had happened without my noticing, or re-membering when, how, or why. I knew that I was different from my old self and had no choice but to commit to a new lifestyle.

Interestingly, many religions claim just such an ex-perience. Christians may say that the Holy Spirit is capable of changing a person instantaneously, and for the better. Many other faiths can claim simi-lar powers of effect. And all of them can point to verifiable examples. My experience could fit nicely within the boundaries of their dogmas. Does my ex-perience then prove the legitimacy of them all?

I will reserve my opinions about their claims for an-other time, possibly that is a different book?

But without regard as to what changed me, I com-mitted. That commitment included several "avoid-ance" behavior modifications, as well as several life-style changes that were "inclusions." Those lifestyle changes on a large scale seemed to be imperative, must-adopt, behaviors.

To demonstrate how sweeping the change was, I have included a list of the primary differences:

These included:
-giving up pot
-giving up tobacco
-giving up cigarettes
-giving up alcohol
-adopting a non-dogmatic vegetarian lifestyle
-stopping driving a car whenever possible
-stopping swearing
-suppressing immoral thinking
-suppressing negative thinking
-suppressing anger
-adopting healthy physical habits
-adopting healthy mental habits
- embracing robust emotional health

Yes, it was a long list. But that didn't deter my commitment. The changes seemed inevitable. Almost like I had no choice in the matter. It was like being reprogrammed, or hypnotized to act in new ways that just a few short weeks before then, would have been impossible to achieve.

I remember within a day or so of the decision to pursue my new lifestyle riding into town to buy food. A brisk, but not too cold, spring morning. I picked up some fruit to eat early in my new vegetarian life. It was a sunny day, no clouds, the sun low in the morning sky. There was water on the streets from the snow melting along the roadside. People were out bustling around shopping, that kind of bustling you see when winter is receding, and spring has not quite yet arrived in a northern midwest town.

I returned home exhilarated from the ride and the idea of fueling it all with fresh fruit. Was it the lack of pot, nicotine, and caffeine, that opened my senses to the great feeling I had after an aggressive bike trip on a chilly Michigan spring day? It didn't matter. I knew that this was the new me.

I was all in.

BLACK DOT

Although I was already in top physical condition, I was dealing with one physical issue that had appeared after the camping trip. And it was a weird one.

On top of my right foot, about midway between the big-toe and the ankle, was a sore, quite bothersome. It was a very tender and quite painful issue. I couldn't remember exactly when it had appeared, and that lack of memory was in itself troubling.

Was it the result of an injury during the bicycle trip to Bay City? Or a more recent wound? I was always worried about skin cancer, and this was a jet-black sore. So black that I thought it might have been a circle of blackened-blood, and upon examination, I confirmed just that! It looked like a plug of skin had been removed, and the wound filled with blood. It was perfectly round. It was just a little smaller than a standard wooden pencil's eraser in diameter. Worse of all, it was always overly tender, and if touched or impacted in the wrong way, it hurt a lot.

That little black spot seemed like it didn't change,

ever. There was no redness around it, at all. And when I finally consulted a doctor, he was as mystified as I was regarding what may have caused it to appear. He opted out of a diagnosis reciting the usual "we'll just keep an eye on it."

Three decades later, a possible diagnosis would emerge and would influence my decision to write this book. That's covered a little later, too.

MUSIC TRUMPS LOVE

It was 1975, mid to late spring, possibly very early summer. Last fall's Bay City bicycle camping trip was a memory glued onto the wall of my life for posterity. I was working at a computer center that was about twenty miles from my new basement apartment. I moved there shortly after the Bay City bike trip.

Living in a basement apartment may have facilitated some of the things about to begin happening. There was earth on all four sides of my apartment, on three sides just beyond the walls, on the fourth side just beyond a small utility room on that side. This sub-terrain placement would shield me from much electromagnetic energy. I also did not own a television, and a small stereo system was the only thing other than lights in my apartment that generated any waves of that kind.

Also, there were no windows except a tiny basement-style window in the place, and the whole residence was just a single room, including a small kitchenette area. The little window was in the bath-room, which had a door. So when the bathroom door was closed, turning off the lights gave me a dark environment, entirely underground. While I was not in a Faraday cage, the shielding was much more than I had ever experienced as far as living quarters are concerned.

It was quiet, secluded, devoid of most radiated elec-tromagnetic energy, and dark on demand.

At the job, there was a new receptionist, and she was a cutie. We'll call her Shelly, not her real name, but close enough. I had a crush on her, but always thought she was out of reach. In those days, I didn't have a high opinion of my ability to impress women. Then one day, as I was going past Shelly's desk, she said, to my amazement, "So when are you going to ask me out?" Well, let insecurities be damned, how about right then and there! Chatting, I learned that her dad owned a large auto dealership. And her brother owned a metaphysics bookstore just a couple miles from my new apartment. That bookstore would eventually figure prominently in my world.

Shelly and I went out a few times. But when I took her to a club to hear one of my favorite local per-formers, she wouldn't stop talking during the per-formance. So loudly that those around were becom-ing irritated at her interrupting the show. I soon came up with a reason to leave that place, and I took her home.

How could I have a relationship with a woman who didn't understand that talking so loudly while sitting in the first row seats at a performance was just wrong? Admittedly I was an idealistic 25-year-old, and I couldn't date a person who would act that way. Or more accurately, I wouldn't. She was hot but loud. So ended the relationship.

But, it was just the beginning of my relationship with the bookstore her brother operated.

THE BOOKSTORE

My new healthy, positive, clean lifestyle was still fresh, and I had added walking to my cycling as a form of travel and exercise. One weekend I decided to walk to the bookstore Shelly had mentioned that her brother operated. It was a Saturday, early afternoon. The walk was a little less than an hour, about forty-five minutes as I recall.

The bookstore was a tiny little place, sitting on the main Detroit artery, Woodward Avenue. Entering you could not avoid the reasonably strong scent of incense, usually a frankincense aroma. It was a little stronger than I preferred, but I liked the smell just the same. The place had the aroma, clientele, lighting, product, and most of all, vibe, to instantly become a permanent memory.

On my first visit, the brother-owner was busying himself by adding some books to his shelves, and I took a moment to introduce myself as a coworker of his sister. He was polite, friendly, but otherwise unimpressed. I politely excused myself and began to explore the place.

It was 1975. Hardly anything at all like the atmosphere today in terms of new-age and metaphysics thinking. In those days, discussion of much of the books' subject material cautiously occurred. Much of it not included in regular social talks. Often the subjects were better referred to as "occult," and the term had a negative connotation. For those in-the-know the store, the "occult bookstore" was just a storehouse of otherwise hidden knowledge. Nothing wrong with that. Fair enough for the times.

Today, difficult to find "occult" subject-material from the 1970s is available at Amazon under the heading of "enlightenment" or in the self-improvement section at Barnes and Noble. But in 1975 the Mayflower Bookstore was very much an occult, that is a, a spiritual and metaphysics hidden knowledge, bookstore frequented by a nearly underground sort of clientele.

Something inside of me was excited to be there. I found myself enthused by all of the books and the 'underground' subjects found there — many of the books imported from Europe or England. The imported books were evidence of Europe's and the UK's advanced state when compared to the U.S. publishing these materials. Study and acceptance of the subject matter were years ahead of the United States at that time. I would eventually become a regular repeat customer and spend a lot of time and money at the Mayflower.

But today was my first visit, and I thumbed through many books that piqued my interests. Suddenly one book virtually jumped off the shelf at me. Why? I have no idea. I immediately purchased it and tucked it into the bookstore's little white plastic bag. I exited the store and began walking home.

It was a beautiful day, and the sun was about 45 degrees above the horizon. It seems like it was about 5 p.m. When I was about 15 minutes from home, I decided to crack open the book and read a little while I finished my trek to my apartment.

My life was about to make a huge turn.

FIRST AHA

This my first book from the Mayflower Bookstore, was titled "Journeys Out Of The Body" by author Robert Monroe. First edition. I opened it to a random page as I was walking in the hot direct late afternoon sunlight. I question if the selected page was indeed "random" or not. Unfolding before me was the first time something in a book would refer to an event the same as an unexplained event in my own life, and consequently change its course.

The random page I opened too interpreted one of my life experience mysteries. Robert Monroe was explaining how some events during out of body experiences, or OOBEs, sometimes included his becoming entangled with physical objects!

Oh! What? I reread the section. And then again.

Oh my gosh. This guy was describing in detail what I had experienced when my hand got entangles with my alarm clock some years before.

I cannot give enough gravitas to the experience of reading about Monroe's episode. I had always wondered if I was having some form of a dream, and if not, then what the experience was exactly. My experience had full consciousness attributes but wasn't the same form of consciousness I usually associated with an "awake" state of mind.

I had wondered if I the only person who had ever had this experience, or similar experiences? Here was another person fully describing their same experience replicating mine. The validation for me was enormous.

I would read Monroe's book several times, and return to the Mayflower bookstore many times, and buy many many books.

The impact of Robert Monroe's book was immense. Suddenly I found myself wanting to know if other experiences I had in my life were also known to others. And that propelled me to return to the bookstore armed with a newfound interest that was fueled by intense curiosity, high levels of energy, and excitement I had not experienced before.

Thus began a series of incredible events over roughly the next two years that would influence the course of my life for the next three decades. I would find out thirty years later, that they may not have been what they seemed at the time they were occurring. But that revelation would require time, for science to catch up.

The thread that ran through my life and included the experiences from my childhood and beyond had persisted inwardly. Hidden away were unrealized, unasked, and unanswered questions; until I found that first book. And then I had confirmation that my experiences were not singular and that others had had similar experiences.

It was as if the truth about the world around me, was known to others who had written books. And if those books were inside the Mayflower bookstore, then I wanted more of that truth.

I started reading books from Mayflower, and that thread of memories came alive within me. I couldn't explain it then, but I knew something important was happening.

There was a change occurring from the inside out, fueled in part by the bizarre, incredible, and beautiful experiences that began to unfold inside my tiny basement apartment. I will attempt to explain both the changes inside of me and the experience I was having within.

THE JOURNEY

Over the upcoming months and years, I bought and read a plethora of materials. An incomplete list would include writings of Rudolph Steiner, Max Heindel's Rosicrucian titles, as well as works from the Golden Dawn, and many branches of Yoga. Theological studies contained, among others, the Book of Mormon, several versions of the Bible, Biblical Hebrew, and Buddhism, Zen, Islam Judaism, and Christian Theology, primarily focusing on prophecy related books and studies.

One of my most pursued studies was of the Jewish Kabalah, and at a time long before today's highly stylized modern Kabalah books were written. Two Rabbis told me that no man should attempt to study Kabalah until they had reached the age of forty years. I was twenty-five, and already into the study of path-working and reading the Zohar myself.

My library grew to over 300 books covering a large portion of the world's religions, and a broad swath through the field of metaphysics. From the time I started studying, I continued to exercise my commitment to living a 'clean life' as I've described it earlier.

I became extremely focused at work and highly productive there as well. My boss, a born-again Christian, didn't quite know what to make of me. I had been a fellow who he initially felt compelled to keep an eye on, and he watched me turn into the equivalent of an urban monk. I'd become mystic minded; a clean living spiritual student at age 25 who lived like a Tibetian monk in the middle of metropolitan Detroit.

Then things in my personal life started to happen that initially were most bizarre.

I do not remember exactly how, or when it all started, but I have no problem recalling the events that began occurring.

MAGICAL
MYSTICAL TOUR

I began to have experiences that I initially referred to as "visions in my sleep." I didn't have a word other than "vision" to distinguish them from dreams. I did not and still do not, think I was dreaming. But I don't think they fit the strict description of visions either. So I will stick with the term vision for now, too.

These "visions," like dreams, occurred while I was sleeping, but they did not otherwise share any dream-like attributes with dream-states. They seemed to be a form of consciousness that was almost as real and sometimes 100% as real, as my waking state. Most of the time, the experiences during the "vision" state were, upon awakening, as real as the waking state itself. I remember thinking that maybe they were both equally authentic, just different.

So, what experiences were occurring?

THE
EXPERIENCES

I had these vision-like experiences often. Eventually, it became the norm to have them almost nightly. At times it seemed unusual if I didn't experience them. Normal, regular dreams, also occurred during that part of my life.

Frequently I would find myself in locations more than once. Not unlike visiting a town more than once. Just as one might be in the same area within the city as you were on an earlier visit, or you might be in the same town, but in a different part of the municipality. Returning to a place I had been to before was remarkable.

That happened quite often. I recall visiting several places many, more than once.

A first location I visited was the neighborhood where I grew up. I was there a few times, on "my street." It had changed, new buildings were in some areas. Later I visited the place, while on a business trip, and confirmed much of what I had experienced in the vision-like event.

There were also places where I found myself so frequently that I knew my way around like it was a place I was familiar with in the here-and-now. So much, I would find myself there, and I could decide where to go and what to do. It was not the same as lucid dreaming. Lucid dreaming was always a challenge for me. But these familiar locations and self-directed travels were fluid and natural.

On one visit, while walking down the street, an odd phenomenon occurred. It was as if something was falling from the sky above me, sort of like light rain. But in this case, the falling "things" couldn't be seen, but as they got a few feet above me, they would pop, like a tiny firecracker. They were loud and very bothersome, although not harmful. I recall ducking into a storefront until the 'storm' stopped; then I continued down the street. That happened a couple of times and always was rather irritating.

Often I regularly found myself in two or three 'neighborhoods' that eventually became familiar. Those had a feel to them when I visited, not unlike the feeling when returning to our home-town from an extended time away.

The modern quantum theory could have a lot to say about this next event. I found myself in front of a home with the front door opened. I entered. I was in a location I had not been to before. Directly inside the front door, there was a wide carpeted staircase. I walked to the right and found that the house layout took me around the stairs, through a couple of rooms, and full circle back to the front door. Once I had completed that circular walk, I was back at the staircase. Looking upward, and at the top of the stairs were a few people. I intuitively knew they were people I loved. Then I left the house.

That experience took place in 1975. In 1978 I met a young woman whom I married in 1980. By 1997 we had been blessed with three children, and we were shopping for our first home.

Our realtor showed us several houses, and upon entering a large two-story home in Vancouver, Washington, we were standing directly in front of a wide staircase. We walked to the right, and through the house, circling the stairs. We went through a few rooms and back to the entryway at the foot of the staircase.

I immediately realized I was inside the home I had visited in 1974, in the "vision." We bought the house. It wasn't long before it was common to see the family I loved, at the top of the staircase.

Here is another. It includes a recurring place that I went to more than once that also had a feeling of familiarity, and which eventually was familiar in the "real world."

In some visions, I would find myself in a high-desert

area. In those visions, someone in my family owned a home there, and I would visit it. It was a little confusing because some of the furniture and furnishings inside the house belonged to me, but I didn't live there. And I didn't know who lived there, but it was family.

However, a short drive, say, 1,000 feet away, there was a newer structure, and that was where I lived, but it always felt like I was still moving-in, or recently had done so. Again, the vision occurred while I lived in Detroit in 1975, and while in the basement apartment.

Now let's jump forward in time to 2016. That year I moved to a new home in the high-desert of California. About 1,200 feet away, my son lives with his family, and his home contains some of the furniture and other items received from my wife and me.

Looking at that desert location from the visionary experiences of 1975, the home we built in 2015-16 mimics the 1975 visions' lay of the land in the real world in many ways. Was the 1975 experience a foreshadowing of the location of both my son's home and my retirement home, nearly 50 years later? It seems so, to me.

This is an excellent spot to pause and let me point out a subtly of writing this book. Most of the incredible events written about were impossible when they occurred. They may have been weird, frightening, unusual, or whatever. But regardless they also were all unexplained. And, the only robust general explanations at that time usually signified systems of religious thought. Those explanations for some of these events may be complete, and valid. However, now we know that those traditional explanations may be correct, and also correct may be other parallel explanations. The new-news is that both are likely correct, the conventional spiritual views, and the new quantum physics views. I urge you, rethink those things that are so close to your heart but always have significantly remained veiled from your mind. We have insights now that might be helpful for you. I have included a reading list at the end of the book to provide a finger pointing the way to new knowledge.

Writing this book might convince someone, even you, to rethink those events in your life that have remained unexplained. New possible answers that you find will bond with your preexisting explanations that are true. You'll "know 'em when you see 'em."

Here is a little event, socially awkward to describe. When it occurred, I was aware that the experiences I was having were not merely vivid dreams. But at the time of this next one, I was confused as to what they were, exactly. When this vision and event I describe had closure, there was little doubt in my mind about their energy source. I realized it was the conscious universe itself that it was "will" and a benevolent will at that.

As I said, it's a little weird, but here it is.

I had a vision that I was standing at a urinal, and was doing what men do there. Looking down into the urinal, all of a sudden, the urinal ran red with blood. But that wasn't the weird part. What was strange was that at the moment I realized that the red flow was blood, I had a great sense of emotional well being! The experience abruptly ended. I was awake.

I mused over how odd it was that the moment that blood had filled the urinal, a great sense of relief overcame me. That made no sense to me at all. I expected that the sight of blood in that context would have been the cause for great fear. But instead, there was a very distinct sense of well being.

Then, two days later, my dad called me. He explained that two days earlier he'd been diagnosed with a kidney stone. Then, the next day, as he was relieving himself, he had passed the stone. He said the passing caused a lot of blood to flow into the urinal. Although the passing had caused the blood flow, the good news was, the stone was gone! The pain was gone, and the need for surgery eliminated — time for a great sense of well being.

Coincidence? Maybe. And maybe not. Premonition? I think so — at least premonition.

This next episode leaves little doubt.

"EXCUSE ME, BUT THE UNIVERSE IS CALLING"

It was one of the outings where I had to drive. Even though I wasn't driving to work, as part of my stress-reduction lifestyle, occasionally I did have to drive. And going shopping was one of those times.

Returning home from shopping, I parked my car, which was brand new at the time. It was parallel to the curb in front of my basement apartment, about 3 feet in front of another car. I parked on a semi-commercial road, although a residential street, it was also a well-traveled road.

Once inside my apartment, I had an overwhelming impulse to go outside and move my car forward about thirty feet. Why? I have no idea now, and I had none then whatsoever. But the urging would not go away, so after a while, I went back outside and pulled my car forward about 30 feet.

The next day I went outside, to my utter amazement, the most incredible sight greeted me.

Overnight a drunk driver plowed into the rear of the car that had parked precisely in the location where I had initially parked my car before moving it. The collision had pushed the impacted car forward about twenty-five feet. It came to rest about five feet from the rear of my vehicle.

Another coincidence? Well, if this was the first possible coincidence, I might say "yes". But it was not the first by a long shot. And by that time my opinion was that these were not coincidences at all.

JEWELED SCRIPT

By now, I had settled into a rhythm of sorts around my new life of clean living and clean thinking. I continued to study all things metaphysical and many things theological, but I had pruned the subject matter somewhat. Moreover, I continued to struggle with the small black, very painful sore on my foot. It didn't get worse, but it also didn't seem to heal.

Initially, some of the material I was reading was pretty far out there. Being a bright guy, I had started to omit some of the books from my study if they just seemed sensational or flaky. It wasn't necessarily that the subject matter was determined to be useless, but the authors had established their writings as merely not useful to me in the slightest. So they were dropped.

For a variety of reasons, I zeroed into the Judeo Christian literature, of many types and varied sects to be sure, but the materials had a uniqueness to them. Primarily I was impressed with how all the religions I had studied required man get himself to God. Whereas the Judeo-Christan tradition clearly showed God getting himself to man, especially in the Christian traditions, a solution to god-man reconciliation that was one-of-a-kind, even to this day. The uniqueness, initially, wasn't so much limited to that observation alone. There was also the experiences I was having while studying the materials.

For example, I can recall that on several occasions, while reading some of the source material, the words on the page seemed to take on a vibrancy hard to explain. It was almost like the words had self-contained energy that flowed outward from each word as read. At times there seemed to be multi-levels of meaning and interpretation to many passages. In short, often the material seemed to come alive with a vibrancy that did not occur while reading most if any, other stuff.

This 1975 occurrence might be the most significant event of them all. It is undoubtedly the primary one that affected my world views profoundly. It also shares something in common with the previous discussion about the words having energy. Although the two experiences are different, there seems to be something in common behind the two. Immediately after the event, I was significantly affected physically, mentally, emotionally, and even spiritually. The incident continues its residue on my beliefs some forty years later.

I had fallen asleep on the floor of my apartment, facing downward. I didn't have a bed, but I did have a mattress, on the floor. That was my bed. However, this particular evening, I was laying on the bare floor, reading, and I had fallen asleep. It is sporadic and uncommon for me to fall asleep accidentally, but I did so on that occasion.

Then, a voice behind me abruptly awakened me. It was the second time I had encountered that voice. It wasn't a voice made up of soundwaves as such. Maybe it was received telepathically in my head; I don't know for sure. But it was the very same kind as the voice that had spoken to me while on the craft. Perhaps it was the very same person's or entity's voice that spoke when I was in the vehicle described earlier during the camping trip to Bay City. It "sounded" and seemed like the same one.

The voice said most effectively, "Wake up," and I did.

To my surprise, I was still lying flat on my stomach. I was apparently in the vision state I had experienced so many times before. This time I was still in my apartment and had raised-up to rest on my forearms looking downward immediately in front of me.

To my surprise and total amazement, directly in front of me lay what looked like a perfect blue rectangular smooth stone tablet of some sort. It was baby-powder-blue similar in color to a container of Johnson & Johnson brand baby powder. It was about 10-11 inches top edge to bottom edge, and 18-20 inches wide, and it seemed to be about an inch thick.

On the top surface, and running left-to-right were multiple lines of what seemed to be a script — evidently writing of some kind. And, interspersed throughout the writing were what looked like several types of precious stones. The stones seemed to be part of the script, a sort of punctuation or so it seemed.

The voice, as in Bay City, remained unseen and behind me, said to me "Read." I assumed this meant for me to read the writing on the tablet. I could not, of course.

I somehow responded with "I cannot."

It seemed as if I said (whatever "said" meant at that moment) that "I cannot because I don't know how to read this language."

No sooner had I conveyed my reply to the command to read, than "he" physically, and ever so gently, but deliberately, touched the back of my head and pressed if gently forward, and down towards the tablet.

To my absolute and utter amazement, in a singular moment of understanding and comprehension, I began to read the script on the tablet!

I remember vividly the shock I was experiencing with my ability to read that thing as quickly as if it were in plain English. The reading was so easy and fluid that I immediately forgot about my amazement and just proceeded to begin reading the thing!

Then the most miraculous thing happened- an experience to last a lifetime.

As I read along with the text, I came, naturally, to the first jewel or gemstone, and when I did, it was as if a massive amount of information streamed out, or more accurately gushed out, from that jewel directly into my mind! There was something similar to a stream of light that seemed to carry the information along into my brain. And that information transfer occurred each time I encountered another precious stone embedded into the script.

I continued to read the script. The experience was like reading anything else until I encountered the next stone. Then, my mind would flood with an enormous amount of knowledge. The influx occurred in bursts that lasted only a few fractions of a moment.

I read until I had exhausted the text. In an instant, I was fully awake, still leaning forward on my forearms, head in the same position as when reading the tablet. Seamlessly, I was back to a waking state of consciousness.

Speechless. Stunned. Overpowered. Enlightened. Blessed. The event had ended. I was overwhelmed with emotion and began to weep. I felt so full of joy and happiness, unlike any experience before or after, in my entire life.

It took several days for the feeling of emotional well being and joy to begin to dissipate. It took many many days, perhaps a week and a half to two weeks for me to return to anything close to my baseline emotional state.

The blue tablet experience was truly life-changing, but not all events were that powerful. Many were just fascinating, less impactful, but noteworthy.

One of these was the experience of effortlessly swimming on my back from Detroit, out from shore to places that seemed far away, but I never actually arrived at any particular location. The experiences reoccurred at least half a dozen times, sometimes with minor variances. It would take decades before those experiences would yield an interpretation.

Many years later, I had the conviction that my extensive business travels were foreshadowed by those repeated swimming experiences away from my home town. Maybe only a convenient association, or perhaps an actual interpretation of another, less critical, premonition.

Rethink some of your less important unexplained events. FInding new possible explanations that satisfy the mind, while not offending the soul, may be good things to add to the review of one's life experiences.

FULLY AWAKE

One such event happened when visiting a married couple who were two of my closest friends. We first met in my "hippy days" a couple of years earlier. They were respectful of my new-found clean life-style, but they continued to drink and smoke while I visited socially.

One evening I was visiting them. As the woman spoke, a glow emerged around her. In sympathy with her emotional disposition, this glow, or aura, would change color and increase or decrease its density and distance from her body.

That was the only time I ever saw what I presumed to be an actual aura, but it was an experience that has remained vivid for me to this day.

I had a similar event a few weeks later. A dear friend whom I had been close to my whole life, an uncle who was only six months different in age, asked me to go out for an early afternoon beer. Of course, I wasn't drinking, but I agreed.

Being a worldly-minded bachelor, he wanted to go to the local exotic dancer bar. I was a little conflicted because I had spent many previous months in my new lifestyle, which included thought management. And my version of thought management included diverting my mind from any thoughts I deemed unbecoming a clean-minded positive thought life. So, hanging out in a topless dancing bar seemed to violate that lifestyle. But before my new-found ways, he and I had done so before, and I didn't want to come across as high-browed. Our friendship was significant to me, and I consented.

As we walked into the bar, just inside the doorway and off to my right, was a small table. On top of it, a dancer was entertaining a customer. As we walked in, her eyes and my eyes met. I cannot adequately describe the experience of that meeting of our eyes, but in the briefest moment, we exchanged something that was, for me, massive emotionally.

An unmistakable surge of shame engulfed me. And what made it even more remarkable was that I was not feeling personally ashamed, or any self-shame, in any way. What I was experiencing was simply an intense shame. Was it her shame? I have no idea at all. To be clear, I am not saying that the dancer experienced anything as I did at the moment. But it seemed as though she might have been having a similar experience.

I don't want to hear from readers telling me about my lack of moral superiority or anything like that. I am not judging anyone or any activity taking place in the bar at all. I am only conveying the experience I had at that moment. That's all. I didn't understand it then nor do I now. But there was an absolute emotional transference that occurred instantly.

Increased sensitivities to the world around me became more and more common. And, the vision-like sleep experiences continued as well. I also was gaining in my skill in what we would now call lucid-dreaming. Awkward at first, yes, but I was improving my ability to consciously directing my actions while having a dream, without waking up.

There were benefits from getting better at lucid dreaming. One advantage was that it further confirmed that the vision-like experiences were not dreams. I knew what a vision-like conscious state was like, and I knew what a dream state was.

Then, out of nowhere, and for no reasons I could identify, something began to happen that was extremely disturbing. Little did I know that my extraordinary experiences were about to come to a sudden halt.

INTRUDERS

One night I was falling asleep, about to enter into the vision-like state. I approached the familiar state-of-consciousness, effortlessly, and as usual through no effort of my own.

Then, something unique and new occurred. Something extraordinarily frightening and awkward to describe. Unlike the other experiences, these seemed to happen just on the perimeter of entering into the vision-like state and blocked me from proceeding further.

As I began to obtain the vision-like condition, It was as if my field of vision became blocked by a black rectangular area. It was total blackness. The complete absence of light, it also seemed to be preventing anything from beyond it, from getting to me. It was as if there was a black space in front of me that prevented me from "entering."

That first night I had the experience, there appeared inside the blackness five to seven creatures, looking back at me from the gloom. I could only see their heads, the rest of their "bodies" extending below the perimeter of the darkness.

I know how this sounds, but that is what I experienced. And those beings were extremely menacing.

Imagine a rectangular window into another, room, space, or dimension, through which several very menacing entities are glaring back at you — and wishing you a lot of malice. That was the experience. It was as if everything I was experiencing up till then brought to an abrupt and very intentional halt.

It was as if "they" were communicating to me, "you are not welcome here," and "do not enter here again, or you will be sorry." It was extremely frightening.

It was the same sort of fear I had in the little condemned house. It felt like that, only this time I could see the perpetrators. I could only see their heads.

It was long before anything had ever been published (to my awareness) about menacing aliens or anything like that. These fellows looked humanoid, but not like the kind of alien drawings we see today. Not like the large-almond-eyed "Greys." These were bald, ugly with smaller than human heads.

The thing that bothered me in terms of appearance was how similar they all looked, and moreover, they had what looked like a bloody sweat-like substance covering their heads. And this troubling experience happened every night when trying to fall asleep.

Just as quickly as all of the tremendous vision-like experiences had come into my life, they abruptly, and for no apparent reason, ceased. It was replaced by this terrifying intrusion that occurred every night, every time I began to drift into sleep.

I stopped sleeping. It was terrifying. No matter how tired I was, these "things" were preventing me from sleeping, and it began to take its toll on me, and quickly. I didn't know what to do.

Eventually, I decided to self medicate myself to see if that would change the situation. Out of desperation, I bought some beer. I got drunk, and that night, I was able to fall asleep without the appearance of the intruders. Why drinking denied the intruders access to me, I did not know. But I didn't care. I only knew that I was able to sneak past them and get some rest.

Over the next several weeks it was hit and miss. If I didn't drink, I might get to sleep without the black rectangle and visitors appearing, or maybe not. Eventually, this cat and mouse routine destroyed my clean living lifestyle and for the moment, my metaphysical journey.

Gradually I returned to my old ways. I was not the same person who had begun. My studies continued, but the intensity waned in the aftermath of the intruders' appearance.

It wasn't too difficult to start drinking and smoking again over time. Interestingly the most challenging thing was to restart eating meat. That took over a year to be re-normalized, and to this day, I sometimes still struggle with eating meat.

It was 1976, and I had relegated those remarkable years' experiences to my past. My religious studies continued to a greater or lesser degree over the years ahead. The convictions and beliefs I'd acquired stayed with me and defined a big part of the next several decades of my life. Meanwhile, the vision-like experiences' memories remained, mostly dormant, but always vivid.

AWAITING MY AWAKENING

In 1978 I met the lady who I would marry, and by 1982, we had started raising a family.

Over the next many years, my career would move us across the continent over seven times. I often have considered that the recurring vision-like experience of swimming from Detroit into a vast body of water was a foretelling of my career's many relocations.

The study experiences I had during those basement years, focused on religious and metaphysical studies, coupled with the experiences I had during those years, shaped my world views. I attribute much of my world view to that part of my life.

Those world view and convictions about life were real assets that gave me and my family-raising a central balancing focus, and a set of beliefs, many of which endure today.

But some things began shortly after the basement

years, that was not so good and were present as I raised my family. Sleep paralysis is one, and claustrophobia being another.

Clostphobia seemed to surface soon after my Bay City experience. Shortly after the Bay City bicycle camping trip, I found myself extremely uncomfortable in confined places. It first became apparent when I was riding in the back seat with friends of a two-door sedan, and I could not handle it.

Sleep paralysis began shortly after the black rectangle and intruder experiences of the basement apartment.

Eventually, I decided that all those good things from the basement days were good things from God. And the bad stuff from that period of my life was just weird things for which I had no real explanation. The claustrophobia and sleep paralysis were also, just odd things that a lot of people go through in their lives.

But those explanations would wane over the upcoming years. I began to find others' similar experiences in their lives, which they attributed to very different causes than God and coincidence.

And as for the black dot on my foot that lingered for a very long time. It did eventually heal, leaving a scar in the spot where the wound had been. That scar persists even to this day, decades later.

My career had gone very well, my kids grown, and

I was beginning planning to retire sometime in the next 5-10 years.

My interest in religious studies continued, but eventually, I had exhausted that as an ongoing intense study. But I retained most of my beliefs and world views obtained over the numerous years.

New interests had surfaced around 2009, and that was an interest in the UFO phenomena and the research in the Quantum sciences.

I had always believed that pure science and true religion must eventually converge.

There has been ever-increasing scientific information about quantum physics, and more availability of information about UFOs, alien beings, and abductions, spurred on by increased public awareness and globally relaxed government classification. My interests in all of those topics always were being piqued.

Theory about the convergence of science and religion was gaining acceptance more than at any time in my life.

So, I gradually began to study research into quantum sciences, as well as information about UFOs, alien beings, and abductions. I could not have foreseen those studies would shed new light on my basement-apartment and other events going all the way back to my childhood. But that is what happened over the next several years.

AWAKENING

My interests in UFO and related topics became significant when I watched Dr. Steven Greer's "Disclosure" event. The event was held in Washington DC at the National Press Club, in May 2001. A large number of very respectable persons said they would testify under oath before the U.S. Congress that their UFO experiences were as stated. That impressed me.

I seriously began reading about UFOs, abductions, and quantum science soon after watching Dr. Greer's Disclosure Project.

Soon after that, I completed reading my first books about UFOs, and then one about abduction experiences. Quickly I had read several books on those and many related topics. Because I was also driving a lot, I also purchased an audiobook app for my phone, and I added audio-books to my library.

In the old days of my metaphysics studies, I had acquired a couple of hundred books and read most of all of them. Eventually, I sold most of those around 1985 and began building what became nearly 500 volumes in my religious studies library. That library, too, I sold around 2008.

Now I was onto another study fueled by a compulsion to know more about these new topics. But this time, my library would be lightweight and portable, being nearly 100 percent digital audio files and digital books. My studies accelerated, and soon, I had covered an immense amount of materials.

In my opinion, the number of UFO sightings and related reports cannot all be explained away. And the ongoing relaxing of secrecy and document releases by France, the UK, and Canada all were evidence of something authentic.

Meanwhile, the quantum sciences were bringing to the scientific realm realizations about consciousness, matter, and energy that transcended traditional Newtonian physics. More and more, physics and the sciences were becoming less and less separate from spiritual theories and beliefs.

When in 1975 I read Monroe's book and the section about entanglement with objects, that "aha moment" was beyond any confirmation I had up till that time. Now it was the 2000s, and my new study was suggesting that experiences many years before may have new explanation possibilities. They may have real-world connections to UFO, abduction, and inter-dimensional phenomena. And modern quantum physics supported many of those possibilities.

These new connections between my experiences from 40 years prior and newly published data broke down the walls between faith, belief, and the newly emerging sciences.

I read "Sight Unseen" by the late Bud Hopkins and came across the stories in the back of the book about abductees biopsies. Some had small round skin biopsies takes from their foot. Exactly what had happened to my foot 40 years before.

Reading about that in Hopkins' book was over-whelming. I began realizing that a lot of what I had experienced had been documented in other books. My experiences warranted renewed consideration in light of those readings. And reconsideration as something authentic, something beyond mere dreams, or even just visions.

And increasingly my spiritual and religious beliefs were being born out, and explored, even validated by modern quantum sciences.

The convergence of scientific fact and religious be-lief was happening right before my eyes, and the eyes of the world!

It was this new awaking of possible new explan-ations for so many things I'd experienced that I decided to write this book. To share my story to encourage others with odd life experiences to con-sider them anew, in light of new scientific theories and recently declassified documents from governments around the globe.

Even confused and fragmented memories might benefit from reexamination when reevaluated in light of new information. For example, when I reflect on the Bay City experience, I can not recall clearly about the end of the night preceding going to sleep and having the on-craft experience. I can remember clearly the entire trip, including the morning I awoke to feel drugged, and the on-craft experience of the night before.

What I can not clearly remember is what happened just before I turned in for the night. Back "in the day" when I tried to remember that night, I had no memory of the event whatsoever. That was in 1974, as previously noted.

Then in the late 1990s, I was working in Ft. Lauderdale, Florida. One night I went for a walk on the ocean-front beach. I remember walking along, and it was very dark, with no lights whatsoever. Then coming up along the shoreline was a Coast Guard helicopter.

Initially, I could only see its white headlamp, but soon I realized it had a bright red light on the craft. For some reason, I could not understand at the time I became unbelievably frightened. So badly that I retreated from the beach quickly and returned to my hotel.

That was in Florida, around 1998.

Years later, and even recently, when I tried again to recall the last night in Bay City, I would remember walking on the very dark beach near the campsite. And I seem to recall a red or orange light appearing over the water of the bay, but then that memory gets confused with the Ft. Lauderdale beach walk experience. Both memories would seem to collide, and I wasn't and still am not, able to separate them.

It is precisely the kind of thing that I have read about as I studied the UFO literature. Often persons reporting specific experiences also report lost, confused, or mixed up memories.

Was I frightened in Ft Lauderdale, because of suppressed memories from Bay City? What was deleted from memory, and why? Is it possible that the suppressed memory from my last night in Bay City had something to do with being in some craft?

Maybe I will never know. What I do know is that my recent study of recently published material has opened possibilities that I may never have known if not for the many excellent books and newly released documents.

Studies of UFO and contactee experiences show similar lost memories that later become confused with others. It was, again, this kind of realization that awakened me to the possibility that perhaps I, too, was experiencing that type of confusion.

Recent stories about people having "downloading"

events are not unlike my blue-tablet account. From what I have read, those events referred to as "downloading" are nearly identical to my experience when reading that jewel punctuated script. The massive influx of information experienced when I came to a gemstone, was similar to what others have described as a "download" during alien encounters.

Other people with similar events may benefit from research into the literature I have mentioned.

Another parallel between my life events and new research can is evidenced in my life changes after my return from Bay City. I had an insatiable interest in all things metaphysical resulting in the studies, including materials from the Mayflower bookstore. Some persons report that after some alien, or contactee encounter they had newfound interests, often of a similar kind. Sleep paralysis and claustrophobia also have been noted and written about as after-effects experienced by those with contacts, or abduction stories.

After retiring, I began looking into remote viewing (RVing). There is a possibility that some experiences I had in the basement apartment, were the result of quantum physics similar to those in play during remote viewing sessions.

I had no concept of RVing (in the 1970s, it was still a black op US Army and CIA activity). I could easily have interpreted the experiences as vision-like experiences. The results of my many experiences were not too dissimilar from directed RVing. Stories such as the home with the staircase, and the desert house story, could have been due to physics that today we think may operate in remote viewing.

Today as I continue my studies of these topics, I am convinced that I have had some exceptional life experiences. I used to think that God was providing these experiences in some cases or that I had some gift. Either explanation could be correct; but equally possible is the effects of quantum sciences, or other encounters, that have only recently become documented.

The advent of quantum physics has had its impact on both science and spiritual beliefs. I am convinced that my early-life assertion that there is no conflict between true religion and pure science is more likely to be scientifically discussed now than ever before.

FINAL THOUGHTS

God, consciousness, quantum physics, non-physical sentient beings, all seem to be aspects of one fantastic reality that we are only beginning to comprehend.

Persons involved in science, quantum studies, and the like continue to suggest that Newtonian science seems to be under reconsideration. Science, as it combines scientific rigor, mystical wonder, and quantum physics converge in ways that we could never have imagined 100 years ago. Many of the most respected scientists and spiritualists who have looked into these intersecting topics may tend to agree with that statement.

Noted physicists and luminaries throughout the ages believe there is a collective consciousness and that we can, and do access it. Top researchers and scientists today are now affirming that some part of us survives the death of the body, in a genuine, personal way. These are exciting times to be alive in the here and now.

I have given the reader an extensive collection of life experiences for which I either had no explanation or an explanation rooted in religious-experience or dogma. In some cases, I have drawn a line between the dots found in UFO, abduction, and quantum physics, along with emerging studies of consciousness, with the dots in my life's stories.

Perhaps you too can find interesting parallels between your life and the incredible truths about our universe, being discovered all around us, in many branches of scientific research and spiritual awakening.

Jesus of Nazareth said, "The kingdom of God is within you" and ancient religious texts when speaking of God admonish us to "...be still and know that I am..." Modern quantum theories around consciousness tell us that consciousness may be a portal to many things available during deep meditation, and prayer, as reported by their practitioners.

Quantum science suggests that the bottom layer, if you will, of all creation, is not the sub-atomic quark, or even "strings" as defined in modern string-theory physics. Non-physical consciousness may in fact be the most fundamental thing created, and all matter is derived from it.

Are those truths religious in nature, or are they just good modern scientific hypothesis? Perhaps we will find, as I believe, that they are both.

The back of this book contains a selected reading list. Please understand that the books represent a tiny raction of the available materials in print, not to mention the seeming endless supply of information on the internet.

Also, feel welcomed to go to my website. There you can send me an email, and if you purchase a book title from the website's reading list (which takes you to Amazon), you support a portion of my expenses covering the costs of publishing and having an internet presence.

Thank you for reading *ReThink*!

START YOUR RETHINK & SUGGESTED READING LIST

Your life expereinces will be quinquely your own.

The reading materials that will connect those experiences to the sciences and currently available study materials are multitude.

Below, are a few book titles and authors that I found helpful on my journey of discovery. They are included here as a starting point, to help you determine what other materials might be helpful to your journey of discovery.

The Suggested Reading List

Please go to my website to see the Suggested Reading List for my book "ReThink." If you order any of these books from my website, I recieve a commission, which helps support my writing and related activities. You can view or order each book from my website; you'll find it here:

michaeljomichael.wordpress.com

Journeys Out of the Body
by Robert Monroe

Penetration: The Question of Extraterrestrial and Human Telepathy by Ingo Swann Entangled Minds: Extrasensory Experiences in a Quantum Reality by Dean Radin, Ph.D.

The Stargate Chronicles: Memoirs of a Psychic Spy, The Remarkable Life of U.S. Government Remote Viewer 001
by Joseph McMoneagle

The Children of Roswell: A Seven-Decade Legacy of Fear, Intimidation, and Cover-Ups by Thomas J. Carey, & Donald R. Schmitt
Tell Me What You See: Remote Viewing Cases from the World's Premier Psychic Spy Major Ed Dames, & Joel Harry Newman

The Expanding Case for the UFO
by M. K. Jessup

The Report on Unidentified Flying Objects
by Edward J. Ruppelt

Fact, Fiction, and Flying Saucers: The Truth Behind the Misinformation, Distortion, and Derision by Debunkers, Government Agencies, and Conspiracy Conmen
by Stanton T. Friedman, & Kathleen Marden

The Wisdom of Your Cells: How Your Beliefs Control Your Biology
by Bruce H. Lipton Ph.D.

The Twelfth Planet: Book 1 of the Earth Chronicles
by Zecharia Sitchin

The Alien Abduction Files: The Most Startling Cases of Human-Alien Contact Ever Reported
by Kathleen Marden, & Denise Stoner

A.D. After Disclosure: When the Government Finally Reveals the Truth about Alien Contact
by Bryce Zabel & Richard M. Dolan

Chakras the Mystical Rainbow in You
by Basmati

UFOs and the National Security State: Chronology of a Coverup, 1941-1973
by Richard M. Dolan

Michael J. O. Michael

We Are Not Alone And They Are Not Our Friends–
Hostile Aliens: Cases of Extreme Extraterrestrial
Aggression
By Chet Dembeck

Sight Unseen
by Bud Hopkins and Carol Rainey

Art, Life and UFOs: A memoir
by Bud Hopkins

Mind Trek
by Joseph McMoneagle

Close Encounters of the Fatal Kind
By Nick Redfern

The Mothman Prophecies: A True Story
by John A. Keel

Men In Black: The Secret Terror Among Us
by Gray Barker

They Knew Too Much About Flying Saucers
by Gray Barker

Something in the Woods is Taking People
byStephen Young

The New International Version Study Bible

by Zondervan Press

Author Contact

I hope you have enjoyed this book. And, that you found it informative, and more importantly, encouraging.

If you wish to write to me, please send an email to me here: michaeljomichael@gmail.com

Thank you!
Michael J. O. Michael
September 2019

My website: http:// michaeljomichael.wordpress.com

"ReThink"

The End

Made in the USA
Coppell, TX
31 August 2020